RUINS
IN
REVERSE

WALTER
DERUNGS

modo

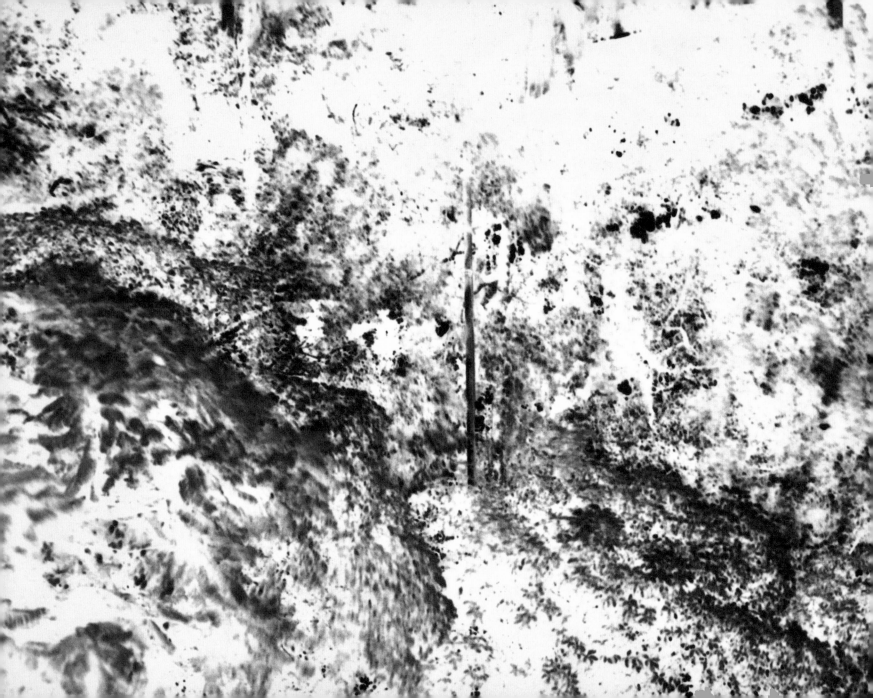

Walter Derungs fotografiert Orte, die durch archi-
tektonische Strukturen definiert sind. Sein Interesse
gilt dabei nicht den Orten selbst, denn die sind
reduzierbar auf ihre Funktion als Standorte, sondern
der Architektur. Anders gesagt dem, was von ihr
übrig geblieben ist. Sein Blick fällt auf Architekturen, die zeitweilig ausser Funktion sind: Verlassene
Freizeitparks, die immer noch auf Besucher warten.
Die Baulücke an *Ground Zero*. Nächtliche Brücken-
pfeiler und Bahnuntergänge. Die nie fertig gestell-
ten Rohbauten, die am ägyptischen Strand wegen
fehlender Investorengelder vor sich hin rotten.
Statt die Funktionalität der architektonischen Strukturen zu thematisieren, hebt Derungs deren bild-
bestimmende Elemente als ästhetische Qualität
hervor und macht sie so zu abstrakten Paraphrasen
ihrer selbst. Es sind die Motive, die dabei im Zen-
trum stehen. Nur selten deutet er Narration und
Temporalität durch die Anwesenheit einer Person
oder mit einem Schattenwurf an. Die abgebildeten
Gegenstände werden zu seltsam deplatzierten,

etwas einsamen ‹Skulpturen›. Die Fotografie isoliert sie in einen Zustand andauernder Gegenwart, wodurch die Dinge sich in ihrer Gemachtheit zeigen: Als stehengebliebene Mauerreste, stillgelegte Unterhaltungstechnologie, falsche Palmen oder wackelige Holzgerüste, und lassen gerade dadurch ihre jeweilige Geschichte erahnen. Derungs hält die Objekte in ihrem verfallenden Zustand, als zeitgenössische Ruinen fest.

In der Motivwahl seiner Orte knüpft Derungs an die stilweisende Autorenfotografie an, deren Hauptvertreter unsere imaginierten Erinnerungen an die Metropolen des 20. Jahrhunderts bestimmt haben. So prägte Robert Franks neugieriger und fremder, da europäischer Blick auf das Amerika der 1950er und 1960er Jahre den Mythos des weiten Westens. Während Frank sich dabei in erster Linie für die Amerikaner interessierte und diese in ihrer Umgebung fotografierte, nähert sich Derungs den dazugehörigen, mittlerweile veralteten, übrig gebliebenen Kulissen und Stätten an. So verwundert es nicht, dass the Parachute Jump, die Ikone des legendären Vergnügungsparks, die bereits in Franks Coney Island, 4th of July 1958 vorkommt, von Derungs in die Serie Vacancy (2007) aufgenommen wurde. Was bei Frank Kulisse für küssende Teenie-Paare am Strand war, inszeniert Derungs nüchtern distanziert als ideale Skulptur im Bild und gleichzeitig liebevoll als Repräsentanten für vergangene Zeiten und ihre Feste. Frank nahm als Fotograf die Position eines Voyeurs ein, nicht selten drehten sich ihm die Porträtierten überrascht zu; sie wurden im Stil traditioneller Fotoreportage ‹auf dem Sprung› festgehalten. Derungs dagegen nähert sich behutsam aus dem Heute den seit damals übrig gebliebenen, menschenleeren Relikten. Das einzig Flüchtige, was er dabei festhält, ist der gegenwärtige Zustand des Zerfalls und damit die kaum bemerkbare, den verlassenen Architekturresten jedoch unweigerlich eingeschriebene Vergangenheit.

Die Arbeit *Müllheim* (2008) ist neu für die Ausstellung *Raumgreifend* entstanden. Sie vereint eine Reihe fotografischer Kompositionen, aufgenommen an sogenannten ‹Nebenschauplätzen› des Städtchens. Hier richtet sich Derungs' Interesse auf Mauervorsprünge, Balkonbalustraden, zugemauerte Fenster, Holzhaufen, beschmierte Unterführungen, aber auch auf die periurbane Umgebung, wie Felder, Büsche und Bäume vor weitem Horizont. Nebensächlichkeiten, die nicht repräsentativ für das offizielle Müllheim sind, sondern Stellvertreter für den vor Ort gelebten Alltag. Die Gebäude und Objekte stehen dabei nicht in der Bildmitte, stattdessen rücken sie bis an den Rand. Derungs offeriert uns einen subjektiven Blick auf eine hiesige, uns vertraute Gegend, in der er sich als Fotograf wie in der Fremde bewegt. Die Bilder dieser Serie wirken im Vergleich zu früheren Arbeiten als wäre der Sucher von Derungs' Kamera auf dem Spaziergang durch Müllheim leicht verrutscht. Als erlaubte die Tatsache, dass es sich dabei um vertraute Objekte und Situationen handelt, ihm einen scheinbar weicheren, etwas lässigeren Blick. Tatsächlich sind die Aufnahmen dieser Serie keine Schnappschüsse, ebensowenig wie die anderen Arbeiten von Derungs, sondern präzise inszenierte Fotografien. Von Bedeutung ist bei *Müllheim* aber auch die Präsentation als Diaschau, jener mit der Banalität kleinbürgerlicher Klischees beladenen fotografischen Vorführform, wodurch sich die Bilder in den Ausstellungsraum ausdehnen und beinahe räumlich begehbar werden. Derungs fordert die Betrachter dadurch auf, seinen Spazierweg durch Müllheim mitzuverfolgen, um die jeweiligen Standorte selbst zu identifizieren. Er lenkt den Blick auf die formalen, skulpturalen Qualitäten der provinziellen Szenarien, die ihrerseits immer von der eigenen Geschichte geprägt sind und deren latentes immer-schon-vergangen-Sein durch die nostalgische Präsentation in projizierter Form zusätzlich verstärkt wird.

Einen neuen Schritt geht Derungs in der Serie urbaner Architekturfotografien *Ruins in Reverse* (2008). Die fotografisch glatten Oberflächen der grossformatigen «Negativabzüge» (Derungs) sind durch den manuellen Entwicklungsvorgang gebrochen und weisen beinahe malerische Schwamm- und Pinselspuren auf. Derungs manipuliert die Abzüge in der Dunkelkammer zusätzlich, indem er Partien ausspart oder zeitlich verzögert zum Entwickeln bringt. Die abgebildeten Gebäude erscheinen dadurch in seltsam kontrastreichem Licht, gleichzeitig sind sie so verfremdet, dass sie zu geisterhaften Erscheinungen werden. Durch die am Bild vorgenommenen Eingriffe ist nicht mehr deutlich zu erkennen, in welchem Zustand die dargestellte Architektur aufgenommen wurde. Die Hochhäuser verlieren ihren stabilen, ikonischen Charakter. Derungs entblösst sie durch den Hinweis auf Fragilität und labile Statik in ihrer Endlichkeit. In der paradoxen Situation von möglicherweise eben erst fertiggestellt und gleichzeitig bereits verfallend, werden sie zu «einstürzenden Neubauten» (Derungs). Zeitlichkeit und Vergänglichkeit, die in anderen Arbeiten von Derungs als Stimmungen mitschwingen, werden in *Ruins in Reverse* tatsächlich dargestellt. Die Unheimlichkeit zeitgenössischer Ruinen manifestiert sich hier nicht mehr bloss als Gefühl, sondern als beinahe verifizierbares, visuelles Phänomen. Gleichzeitig lässt der Titel der umgekehrt gepolten Ruinen auch auf andere, surreale Kräfte schliessen: Die Gebäude befinden sich im Bau; sie werden wie von Geisterhand gebaut. Ohne dass der Verfall Überhand nimmt, könnten Ruinen ohne unser Zutun zu Architekturen werden. Zu Orten, an denen neue Feste gefeiert werden.

MAJA WISMER
BASEL, IM MAI 2008

Walter Derungs photographs locations that are defined by their architectural structures. His interest is not centered on the places themselves, for they are reducible to their function as sites, but on the architecture. Or, put differently, what is left of it. His gaze falls on architecture that is temporarily out of order: deserted amusement parks, still waiting expectantly for visitors. The gap left at *Ground Zero*. Nighttime bridge piers and railway underpasses. The shells of buildings that rot away on the Egyptian beach for lack of investment funds. Instead of thematizing the functionality of the architectural structures, Derungs highlights their image-defining elements as an aesthetic quality and turns them into abstract paraphrases of themselves. It is the motifs on their own that stand center stage. Only seldom does he hint at narration and temporality by the presence of a person or a cast shadow. The pictured objects are turned into strangely displaced, somewhat solitary 'sculptures'. Photography isolates them in a state of the enduring present, whereby the things show themselves in all their 'constructedness': as leftover wall remnants, inoperative entertainment technology, artificial palms or shaky wooden scaffolding, so that the history of each can thus be conjectured. Derungs has captured the objects in a state of decline, as contemporary ruins.

In his choice of motifs and sites, Derungs goes back to the pioneering auteur photography, whose main representatives have defined our memories of the metropolises of the 20th century. Thus Robert Frank's curious and outsider (because European) view of America of the 1950s and 1960s helped mold the myth of the endlessly expandable West. While Frank was at first interested in the Americans as subjects and photographed them in their surroundings, Derungs eventually drew nearer to these accompanying, in the meantime, leftover and out-

dated backdrops and scenes. It is no wonder then that the *Parachute Jump*, the icon of the legendary amusement park that had already turned up in Frank's *Coney Island, 4th of July 1958*, was included in Derungs' *Vacancy* series (2007). What for Frank was a setting for kissing teeny-boppers at the beach, Derungs, in his picture, stages the Jump soberly and distanced as ideal sculpture and at the same time lovingly, as representative of past times and their festivities. As a photographer, Frank took up the position of a voyeur and often the people he portrayed turned round to him in surprise; they were snapped 'on the go', in the style of traditional photo-reportage. Whereas Derungs approaches carefully from today's relics that have, since then, become deserted remnants. The only ephemerality that he holds to is the present state of decline and, with it, the hardly noticeable past that is yet inevitably inscribed in the deserted architectural remains.

The artist has finished his new work *Müllheim* (2008) specifically for the exhibition *Raumgreifend* (space-filling). It brings together a series of photographic compositions taken at so-called 'small-time' city locations. Derungs interest here is focused on wall ledges, balcony railings, shuttered windows, wood piles, scrawled-on underpasses, but also on the urban outskirts such as fields, bushes and trees against a broad horizon. Minor issues that are not representative of official Müllheim but are stand-ins for everyday, local life. The buildings and objects are not placed center stage, but shifted to the margins of the photo. Derungs offers us a subjective view onto a local quarter that is familiar to us, where he as photographer moves through it like an outsider. In contrast to earlier works, the photos in this series seem as if the viewfinder of Derungs' camera was slightly off kilter on his stroll through Müllheim. As if the fact that it is about familiar objects and situations allows him a seemingly softer, somewhat more laid-back view of things. But in fact this series is not made up of snapshots (and neither are the other works by Derungs), but precisely staged photographs. What is significant about *Müllheim* is also its presentation as a slide show, that projection form that is charged with the banality of petit bourgeois cliché, whereby the pictures reach out into the exhibition room and become almost a walk-around space. Derungs thereby prompts the viewers to accompany him on his stroll through Müllheim and identify the sites for themselves. He directs our eyes to the formal, sculptural qualities of the provincial scenarios that, on their part, are always marked by their own history and whose latent always-already-past existence is additionally reinforced by a nostalgic presentation in a slide-projected form.

Derungs goes one step further in his series on urban architectural photographs, *Ruins in Reverse* (2008). The photographically glossy surface of the large-scale "negative prints" (Derungs) are interrupted by the manual developing process and show almost painterly traces of sponge and paintbrush. Derungs has manipulated the prints in the darkroom once again, by leaving out parts or developing them with a time delay. The pictured buildings thus appear in a strange, strongly contrasting light while, at the same time, so distorted that they turn into ghostly apparitions. By means of the interventions in the picture, it is no longer easy to recognize the state in which the portrayed architecture has been shot. The high-rise edifices lose their stable and iconic character. Derungs exposes their finite nature by indicating their fragility and unstable dynamics. In the paradoxical situation of possibly having just now been established and simultaneously already deteriorating, they become "collapsing new buildings" (Derungs). Temporality and transience, which resonate as moods in other works by Derungs, are actually depicted in *Ruins in Reverse*. The eeriness of contemporary ruins are here no longer manifest as just a feeling, but as an almost verifiable, visual phenomenon. At the same time, the title of reversely-polarized ruins can be projected from other, surreal forces: the buildings are under construction; they are being built as if by magic. Instead of the deterioration getting out of hand, ruins could become architecture without any outside help. And turn into places where new festive celebrations can take place.

MAJA WISMER
BASEL, MAY 2008

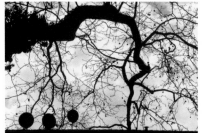

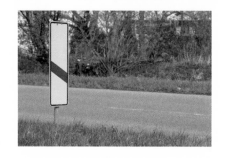

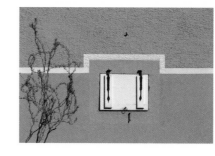

Ruins in Reverse, 2008
02   95 x 117 cm, s/w, Unikat
04–11   117 x 95 cm, s/w, Unikat
12   92.5 x 93 cm, s/w, Unikat
16, 17   117 x 95 cm, s/w, Unikat
08–09, 14–15, 18–19   Detail

Saudade, 2008
20–21   Detail
23   145 x 95 cm, s/w, Unikat
24   95 x 145 cm, s/w, Unikat
26   130 x 95 cm, s/w, Unikat
27   26 x 38 cm, s/w
28, 29   100 x 67 cm, s/w
30, 32   26 x 38 cm, s/w

Müllheim, 2008
Projektion, 80 Farbdiapositive
42–47   Auswahl 46 Stk.

Vacancy, 2007
49   67 x 95 cm, s/w, Unikat
50–52, 55, 58   28 x 40 cm, s/w
53   40 x 28 cm, s/w
56–57   30 x 30 cm, s/w
59   80 x 55 cm, s/w

Alle Schwarzweiss-Fotografien sind vom Künstler handvergrössert.

1970
in Chur geboren

1996–99
Freie Kunstklasse, Bildhauerei,
Hochschule für Gestaltung und Kunst, Basel

1999–2001
Nachdiplom-Studium,
Kunsthochschule Berlin-Weißensee

lebt und arbeitet in Basel
www.walterderungs.ch

2008
Raumgreifend, Markgräfler Museum, Müllheim

2007
1967, Ausstellungsraum Klingental, Basel
Vacancy, Projektraum M54, Basel

2006
Jahresausstellung der Bündner KünstlerInnen,
Kunstmuseum Chur
Regionale 07, Galerie Stapflehus, Weil a. R.

2005
Never-Never, PPS Gallery, Perth, Western Australia
Re-Port, Institut Brasilea, Basel
Kunstkredit Basel-Stadt, Kunsthaus Baselland, Muttenz
Regionale 06, Kunsthalle Basel

2004
Regionale 05, Kunsthaus Baselland, Muttenz
Jahresausstellung der Bündner KünstlerInnen,
Kunstmuseum Chur

2003
Regionale 04, Kunsthalle Basel
Jahresausstellung der Bündner KünstlerInnen,
Kunstmuseum Chur

2002
Take over, Waldhaus Hotels, Flims
Ausstellungsraum restitution, Berlin

2001
Berlin Biennale, *Superchannel*,
mit der Künstlergruppe D.i.A.,
Kunstwerke, Berlin

Modest Proposal, Kunstraum Schweizer National,
Frankfurt am Main
Jahresausstellung der Bündner KünstlerInnen,
Kunstmuseum Chur

2000
Grauer Star – Junge Bündner Fotografie,
Bündner Kunstmuseum Chur
Ausstellung mit D.i.A., Galerie Radio Berlin
Ernte 1999, Liestal

1999
Selection 99, Kunsthaus Baselland, Muttenz
Jahresausstellung der Bündner KünstlerInnen,
Kunstmuseum Chur

2008
Freies Künstlerstipendium, Kanton Graubünden

2006
Förderbeitrag, Foto-Filmkredit, Basel

2005
iaab – Atelieraustauschprogramm,
Fremantle, Western Australia
Werkstipendium, Kunstkredit Basel-Stadt

2003
Förderbeitrag, Foto-Filmkredit, Basel

2001
Freies Künstlerstipendium, Kanton Graubünden

1998
Ebene e / Die Versicherung,
Freie Kunstprojekte, Kunstkredit Basel-Stadt

1996–1997
Projet Kurt, Organisation und Betrieb
eines Off-Space Kunstraumes in Basel,
Freie Kunstprojekte, Kunstkredit Basel-Stadt

Herzlichen Dank an:
Basile Bornand
Elisabeth Büchner-Straumann
Johannes Buchholz
Livie Davatz
Cornelia Dietschi
Jeanne Haunschild
Thomas Hauri
Clare Kenny
Andreas Kreienbühl
Noori Lee
Jan Merk
Gabriela Morschett
Simone Neuenschwander
Nicole Schmid
Dieter Weber
Maja Wismer

Diese Publikation erscheint
anlässlich der Ausstellung
Walter Derungs – Raumgreifend
des Markgräfler Museum
im Blankenhorn-Palais
(17. 07. – 26. 10. 2008)

Herausgeber:
Markgräfler Museum und
Arbeitskreis Kunst Müllheim

Konzept:
Walter Derungs,
9•6 | Conceptional Worlds

Gestaltung:
Nicole Schmid, 9•6 | Conceptional Worlds
www.9--6.com

Lektorat:
Dieter Weber

Übersetzungen:
Jeanne Haunschild

Katalogfotografie:
Basile Bornand, Basel

Gesamtherstellung:
modo Verlag Freiburg i. Br.

Bibliografische Informationen
Der Deutschen Bibliothek
Die Deutsche Bibliothek verzeichnet
diese Publikation in der
Deutschen Nationalbibliografie;
detaillierte bibliografische Daten
sind im Internet über
http://dnb.ddb.de abrufbar

© 2008, Walter Derungs
und modo Verlag, Freiburg i. Br.
für die Texte: bei der Autorin

modo Verlag GmbH Freiburg i. Br.
www.modoverlag.de

Printed in Germany

ISBN 978-3-86833-007-6

Mit großzügiger Unterstützung von: